# SAN LUIS OBISPO
## COUNTY, COAST & CASTLE

Written by Vicki León
Designed by Ashala Nicols-Lawler
with images by 37 of the area's finest photographers*

A PRODUCTION OF

BLAKE
*Graphic Center*

© 1987 Blake Publishing, Inc.
2222 Beebee Street, San Luis Obispo, California 93401
ISBN 0-918303-11-7

*Acknowledgments on inside back cover

# CONTENTS

San Luis Obispo County should carry a warning label. The place is addictive. After a few months of living here, you find yourself bicycling home the long way, blowing foolish quantities of film on whales and butterflies, breaking dates to watch the sunset.

And why not? After all, this is the place where one of the richest men in the world chose to build his castle. William Randolph Hearst loved San Luis Obispo County, and wasn't afraid to say so. And love of place seems to be what has attracted the rest of us as well. This unabashed outpouring of love is, oddly enough, directed at a *county*, a political subdivision so special that its residents regularly hug themselves in secret glee, saying, "How did I get lucky enough to end up *here*?" "County" is itself a dull word, bringing to mind dusty ledgers and courthouses. San Luis Obispo County serves as the shining exception – a 3,316-square-mile parallelogram of terrain along California's tanned midsection. Beautiful, yes, but not (thank God) too prettified. On the golden parchment of its landscape are sprinkled 24 small towns, each one as distinctive as a signature. There's Morro Bay, home to the romantic silhouette of Morro Rock. San Luis Obispo city, the likeable county seat. Pismo Beach, an endless summer of sand dunes and brilliant flowers. The wine country of Paso Robles, honest as a Western saddle. (Plus 20 other villages you're even less likely to have heard of.)

Not just the towns but our natural wonders possess a human scale. Our valleys are snug; our canyons, cuddly. Our graceful mountains invite approach. And it's all accessible, thanks to a 1,200-mile network of back roads – scenic, curvy little numbers, ideal for Sunday morning meandering. (Meandering is also permitted – even encouraged – on Monday through Saturday.)

5

*Farming for flowers: fields near Cambria produce Technicolor crops.*

Besides its impeccable scenery and climate, another fortunate thing has befallen our county: no one can quite identify where it is. Some sources call San Luis Obispo County part of the Central Coast, but few agree as to what *that* is, either. More often than not, the county gets defined by its relationship to other places. Midway between Los Angeles and San Francisco, for instance. We don't mind being "the between place." In fact, we like living in California's best-kept secret; this way, our paradise will stay lost a little longer.

San Luis Obispo, a place whose acronym is SLO. As in the slow life. We're a diverse group, the 193,000 people who live here. But we agree on one thing. We believe that the slow life is the good life. We see San Luis Obispo County as a gathering place for slow folk, for browsers and amblers and saunterers. It's a home for people who prefer the action at the Farmers' Market to that of the stock market. And it's a haven for people – residents and visitors alike – who are more interested in the human race than the rat race.

*Variety is the spice of San Luis Obispo County: tidepooling along the sea-nibbled coast; getting a sunset gander of Bishop's Peak from horseback; photographing the orange flame of local poppies.*

For 8,000 years, this area was the dwelling place of the Chumash Indians, who must have lived a pleasant life: benign climate, quantities of seafood – even hot springs to soak in. Although they periodically rescued the Spanish explorers with their offerings of acorn mush, the Chumash were not agriculturists. It remained for the Spaniards to plant grapes, fruit trees, wheat, corn and beans. And to bring in the nucleus of the great livestock herds which came to dominate the California landscape.

Spanish influence, which began with the founding of the San Luis Obispo mission in 1772, gave way to Mexican rule and then Yankee. By 1850, San Luis Obispo was one of the state's 27 charter counties. It didn't matter whose flag was overhead. Local people just kept on growing things. Today, over 1,400 farms raise economically important quantities of broccoli, barley, celery, lettuce and other crops from sugar peas to flower seed.

*Green power: agriculture remains the county's biggest business. Pictured top right: Farmers' Market each Thursday night in San Luis Obispo city, an event that mixes field-fresh produce with the best free show in town.*

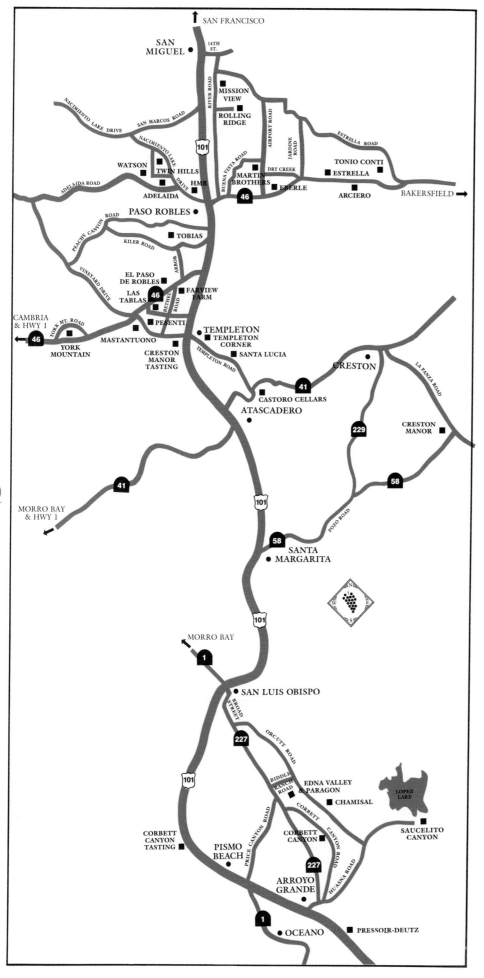

SAN FRANCISCO ↑

14TH ST.

SAN MIGUEL ●

■ MISSION VIEW

RIVER ROAD

■ ROLLING RIDGE

NACIMIENTO LAKE DRIVE

SAN MARCOS ROAD

NACIMIENTO LAKE

AIRPORT ROAD

JARDINE ROAD

DRY CREEK

ESTRELLA ROAD

TONIO CONTI
ESTRELLA ■

101

WATSON ■

ADELAIDA ROAD

■ TWIN HILLS

HMR ■

ADELAIDA

BUENA VISTA ROAD

■ MARTIN BROTHERS

■ EBERLE

46

ARCIERO ■

BAKERSFIELD →

PASO ROBLES ●

PEACHY CANYON ROAD

KILER ROAD

■ TOBIAS

VINEYARD DRIVE

ARBOR

EL PASO DE ROBLES

LAS TABLAS

BETHEL ROAD

46

■ FARVIEW FARM

CAMBRIA & HWY 1

YORK MT. ROAD

46 ←

YORK MOUNTAIN

MASTANTUONO

PESENTI ■

● TEMPLETON

■ TEMPLETON CORNER

CRESTON MANOR TASTING

TEMPLETON ROAD

■ SANTA LUCIA

CRESTON

LA PANZA ROAD

41

■ CASTORO CELLARS

ATASCADERO ●

229

CRESTON MANOR ■

41

58

MORRO BAY & HWY 1 ←

101

POZO ROAD

58

SANTA MARGARITA ●

101

MORRO BAY

1

SAN LUIS OBISPO ●

BROAD STREET

ORCUTT ROAD

227

BIDDLE RANCH ROAD

EDNA VALLEY & PARAGON ●

■ CHAMISAL

LOPEZ LAKE

101

CORBETT CANYON ROAD

PRICE CANYON ROAD

CORBETT CANYON ■

CANYON ROAD

SAUCELITO CANYON ■

CORBETT CANYON TASTING ■

PISMO BEACH ●

227

ARROYO GRANDE ●

HUASNA ROAD

1

OCEANO ●

■ PRESSOIR-DEUTZ

*Winetasting weekends: a growing number of local wineries and vineyards have reached prize-winning maturity. Among those whose wines are worth a weekend trek: Saucelito Canyon, pictured left; Mastantuono, right. If you're looking for more area wineries to explore, get a copy of* **California Wineries:** *a Photographic Profile of San Luis Obispo, Santa Barbara and Ventura Counties, available locally. Its in-depth coverage includes detailed maps.*

10

We don't just live from our agriculture – we view it as
form of entertainment. All year round, there are fairs and
armers' Markets to enjoy. And we mark the turn of the seasons
y exploring farm trails and their bounty – from cider, pumpkins
nd tangelos to strawberries, basil and sweet corn.

Since the 1970s, local ag efforts have tilted toward less
aditional crops: kiwis, citrus, avocados. (And another
icturesque "crop". . . the raising of purebred horses, especially
rabians.) But the biggest trend has been towards the grape.
early 30 wineries and uncounted vineyards have come into
eing, most of them concentrated in two areas. The north county
luster takes in San Miguel, Paso Robles and Templeton. The
ther cluster centers around Edna Valley, just south of San Luis
bispo city. Both are gaining acclaim for superb standards in
rapes and wine, with special crows of delight going to our
infandel, Chardonnay and Cabernet Sauvignon varietal wines.

**Big sky country:** *all over the county SLO cowboys and cowgirls occupy themselves with getting those little dogies along. In Mission days, dried beef was a staple. These days, local beef jerky is a delicacy sold nationwide.*

That wide-open Western feeling is alive and well in San Luis Obispo's cattle country. During the era of the great ranchos (1820s-1860s), the hospitality was as limitless as the horizon. So many rancheros were eager to host rodeos and fiestas that a resolution had to be passed, assigning each of them specific dates. The list for 1850 had 28 rodeos scheduled – in a county whose total population was 336! Twelve years later came the disastrous California droughts. Those two years left the landscape littered with dead animals and foreclosures. San Luis Obispo was fortunate; most of its agricultural land continues as cattle country. And local hospitality remains as big-hearted as in days past. Just follow your nose and the nearest pair of cowboy boots to a savory Santa Maria-style barbecue for a taste of it.

Big skies, Western friendliness, stunning scenery, rural pace – all these things bind our county together. In the pages to come, you'll see and celebrate the differences that have also given our county its character.

# SAN LUIS OBISPO

*Little city of bishops
creek-rich, tree-dappled
you are a necklace of coral and ivory
lightly riding
the soft throat of volcanic peaks.*

*Win, place and show: SLO city attractions include an alluring creek, a creative ferment of artisans and the Fremont, often called the last great Art Deco theatre to be built in the U.S.*

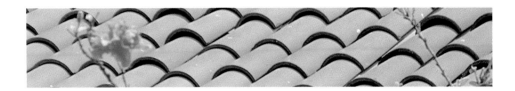

Do your best to ignore those well-meaning folk who tell you to visit the mission or the museum first. If you want to grasp the essential San Luis Obisponess of this place, your first order of business should be to climb Bishop's Peak. You have a choice of routes, both of which run through private property; their owners graciously allow access to considerate climbers. Once past the steep pastureland, the climb gets more vertical and vigorous (but still easy – this is not mountain-climbing, really). You wiggle between boulders, stopping often to gape at the changing views. In less than an hour, you gaze down on the city of San Luis Obispo, its buildings so softened by vegetation that the panorama resembles the tightly curled hair of a boy. The edges of the town end as neatly as a haircut, being prevented from straggling by the foothills. To the east, the hills resemble a collection of knees wrapped in a warm brown Velour blanket. To the west – where you stand – are the rougher, greyer sentinels of San Luis Mountain and Bishop's Peak, seemingly created to provide beautiful silhouettes for the sunset.

There's nothing quite like a San Luis Obispo sunset. First, the sun disappears behind the peaks. Then the sky takes on the purest watercolor wash of color – sometimes violet, sometimes indigo, occasionally the palest gold. Just when you think you've had the full treatment, the fog display begins. Some evenings, a few shy tendrils curl over the peaks. Other nights, a great bank, thick as a comforter, rolls between the mountains. From your vantage point of Bishop's Peak, you can see west along the county's beautiful spine of volcanic peaks to the ocean, where the fog waits in the wings each summer afternoon.

(Other don't-miss locales for peak and sunset ogling are from Cuesta Ridge and from Orcutt Road just south of Islay Hill – see our map inside the front cover for specific directions.)

17

***Community anchor:*** *named for the French bishop of Toulouse, Mission San Luis Obispo de Tolosa has been sitting in the shadow of Bishop's Peak for more than two centuries. In the fashion of missions, it has suffered misfortunes from fire to earthquake, and has been built and rebuilt in a variety of styles and locations. Pictured top: the SLO Bicycle Criterium, a world-class event, has its focus in Mission Plaza, as does the congenial Central Coast Wine Festival, pictured right.*

**Slow pace, fast friends**: *if a prize were given for sheer niceness, the residents of San Luis Obispo – city and county – would walk away with it. That friendliness makes local festivities – such as the Central Coast Wine Festival – extra pleasant.*

A town that grew up around a mission, San Luis Obispo has had a strongly Spanish past. On September 1, 1772, Father Junípero Serra founded the mission and headed south, leaving the small settlement with a quantity of flour, wheat, chocolate and a box of brown sugar. From these modest beginnings, Mission San Luis Obispo de Tolosa grew to become one of the most successful in the 21-mission chain. At the peak of its prosperity, more than 12,000 head of livestock carried the Mission brand. Despite its holdings, the mission sold for a mere $510 when it was secularized in 1835.

Even after California became a state in 1849, San Luis Obispo – both city and county – retained its Latin flavor. Records were kept in Spanish; accounts, in *pesos* and *reales*. The first teachers taught in Spanish (a poll in 1854 found only 40 English-speaking children in the entire county). Curiously, there are few tangible reminders of this Latin heritage. Aside from the mission, you are left to contemplate the c. 1853 Murray adobe in Mission Plaza and the rather unMediterranean façades of the Sauer and Dallidet adobes.

The arrival of the Southern Pacific Railroad into the county in the 1880s gave San Luis Obispo an even more decisive American flavor, a pattern further set by the establishment in 1901 of California Polytechnic State University.

Architectural sightseeing is our forte, appropriate in a city whose university school of architecture ranks among the best in the U.S. Name your favorite – we've got it. Sunny Victorians; charmingly decrepit barns; the stunning Art Deco swan neck of the Fremont Theatre; the Ah Louis store, jade-and-white souvenir of a Chinatown that once numbered 3,000; the granite faces of the county museum and Presbyterian Church; and the rock fantasy of the Madonna Inn.

But the most attractive qualities of San Luis Obispo are unpinnable. Words and photos can do little to capture the honeyed quality of the sunlight. The aromatic wealth of trees that line our streets – camphor and California pepper, jacaranda and redwood. The sound of San Luis Creek, the bright ribbon of water along which locals gather to munch, meditate or listen to music. Its low-key presence is one of the small repeated pleasures of this town.

*Guinness contenders: superlatively speaking, SLO city has three categories covered: most charming old barn; first motel in the U.S. (pictured bottom left c. 1930); and world's most fantastic place to snooze – the Madonna Inn. Its 109 imaginative rooms make lavish use of waterfalls, local stone and art. Room motifs cover every wish fulfillment in the book, from "Caveman" to "Bridal Falls."*

Real towns, like real people, have hearts. Mission Plaza is San Luis Obispo's. An artistic flow of stonework walls, grassy areas, nooks, crannies, fountains, footbridges, flowers and flags whipping between tall eucalyptus trees, Mission Plaza ties the creek, the mission, the Art Center and surrounding restaurants and stores together. So harmonious is the result that few people realize this traditional town heart devoted to pedestrian pursuits is in fact just a few decades old.

There's always something afoot in Mission Plaza. It could be as elaborate as the Fourth of July whingding. At times like this, the Plaza is thronged with people, booths, food stands and balloons, pulsating with live music, dance events and street theatre. Oftentimes, it is something simpler but no less fascinating. A skateboard contest for kids. A wedding at the Mission. Or maybe just three guys playing guitar for the noontime brown-baggers.

San Luis Obispeños will use almost any excuse to throw a celebration. A quick lineup of the major annual events in the city includes: Poly Royal (April), the

*The natives are restless: Obispeños are content where they are but most of them enjoy changing who they are. Festivals let locals become a queen, a medieval cheese merchant, or a bobbysoxer for a day or a night.*

niversity's weekend to strut its echnological and cultural stuff; La iesta (May), the city's tribute to its atin past; the Renaissance Faire June) a full-on Elizabethan romp, lone entirely in period costume and anguage; Mozart Festival week August), a program of top-flight nusicians playing in county-wide ettings as awe-inspiring as the nusic; the Central Coast Wine estival (late August), a chance to ompare the wares of wineries from hree counties; and Mardi Gras February), begun by a core group of happy fanatics, now a citywide evel with a nighttime parade, floats

and imaginatively bizarre costuming and behavior.

These events and dozens of others crowd the city calendar. Despite the competition, the Mozart Festival remains the biggest draw. It matters little if you are a classical music buff. This is an unstuffy week of live performances – musical, artistic and dramatic – held in the city and around the county. The common denominators of the Festival are quality and understandability. Quite like San Luis Obispo itself, really.

During its first 130 years, San Luis Obispo welcomed a succession

*Roots: ethnic groups add sparkle to the events calendar. Among them: the Japanese Obon Festival, the Cinco de Mayo Fiesta sponsored by the Mexican community, and numerous Portuguese celebrations (pictured top).*

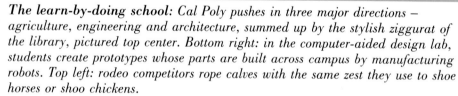

*The learn-by-doing school: Cal Poly pushes in three major directions —
agriculture, engineering and architecture, summed up by the stylish ziggurat of
the library, pictured top center. Bottom right: in the computer-aided design lab,
students create prototypes whose parts are built across campus by manufacturing
robots. Top left: rodeo competitors rope calves with the same zest they use to shoe
horses or shoo chickens.*

of ethnic groups whose names and celebrations still enliven the area: Mexican, Irish, German, Chinese, Swiss-Italian, Portuguese, and Japanese. Since the beginning of this century, the town's growth has not tilted toward any particular ethnic group but rather toward an age group. Between its two institutions of higher learning, San Luis Obispo now has a college student population that represents nearly one-half of its total population.

California Polytechnic State University is a key part of the 19-campus state university system.

Although Cal Poly's emphasis was primarily agricultural in its early years, it has since developed strong schools of architecture, science, math, engineering and business. (Cal Poly's setting is so spectacular that certain students claim to have come here to major in the view.)

Six miles west of the city lies Cuesta College, a two-year community school that almost everybody in town has attended in one capacity or another. Both colleges have performing arts facilities and programs that bring big-city cultural events on a regular basis to San Luis Obispo.

# THE COAST

*A finger of sand at Morro Bay*
*points the way to the cool north coast*
*to the salty brightness of seaside villages*
*to the turquoise kingdoms*
*of sea otter and whale.*

**The coast:** *a hospitable refuge for visitors of all sorts. Pictured left: the 50-year hospitality of the Log Cabins, Morro Bay's first public lodgings, is now history. But the coast still welcomes thousands of migratory birds and people each year.*

With 84 miles of spectacular beaches, this is definitely a coastal county. We locals, however, are just as fond of the coastal backcountry, pierced through and through with dozens of little valleys and mountain ranges.

There are mountains and mountains, but our peaks are paramount. Marching west to the Pacific from San Luis Obispo city are nine extinct volcanoes that came into tempestuous being about 22 million years ago. Also known as "the sisters" for their common origin, the peaks provide the county with its most beautiful necklace of landmarks. Two of the peaks are stubby enough to be called hills. The ninth "peak" sits in the ocean at Morro Bay and is called Morro Rock. (*Morro* is Spanish for any round-headed object or headland. Just to be confusing, we sometimes call all nine peaks "the morros.")

You can gain no finer introduction to the coast than to ramble along the north side of the peaks, following Highway 1. Scenic as it is, don't just follow the highway up the coast. Instead, get a taste of the back country by turning off at, say, Cayucos. One minute, you're looking at the long waves and half-smile of Estero Bay. The next, you're in up-and-down terrain, where pines with great crinoline skirts shade the road. Barely ten miles from Cayucos, you intersect with Highway 46 west and cross to Santa Rosa Creek Road. At this height, the hills and ocean have a Big Sur dreaminess about them. Gradually the road approaches its namesake creek. Berry bushes and family farms appear, some with roadside stands and picnic spots. Five more miles, and you've reached the pines and emerald hillsides of Cambria, where you can join Highway 1 once again.

*What's your sign:* in Morro Bay, it's bound to be pisces. Commercial and sports fisherpeople bring in big-dollar catches of salmon, albacore, crab and 40 species of bottomfish. Protected by The Rock, the harbor gets further sheltering from the 3½-mile-long sandspit, whose steep dunes can be seen to advantage from Pecho Road on the way to Montaña de Oro.

A seaside village with a photogenic fishing fleet and a monolithic crag of a rock in the harbor is in real danger of terminal quaintness. Morro Bay, however, does not have that problem. A billboard that once said "Come see our pet rock" is about as cute as locals get about their town. The waterfront Embarcadero has its share of souvenirs but it also has boat hulls being scraped, fish being cleaned and other real-life activities that relate to the care and feeding of the fishing industry rather than the care and feeding of tourists en masse.

The proof of Morro Bay's realness is the gusto with which residents enjoy their town. Just take a poll of the people out whale-watching, watercoloring the Rock or having a sunset drink on

he waterfront, and you'll come up with a solid core of hometown folks.

A magnificent bird refuge, fog-rich Morro Bay is often the soft grey of cat's fur – which makes the occasional blast of color from its local foliage even more stunning. There are wondrous plantings of iceplant, whose shocking pink flowers carpet the slopes of town. So vivid are the blooms that they can be seen five miles out to sea by the fishing fleet.

In the late 1800s, pioneers such as Frank Riley planted forests of eucalyptus trees. Originally intended to combat the wind and sand, the eucalyptus have become attractions in their own right. Along Morro Bay's main streets, their scarlet flowers make a Christmas-bright display.

*My old flame: one of Morro Bay's favorite events is the annual Firemen's Muster, crowned by a parade of beautiful old engines and rigs.*

**Home sweet estuary:** *66 kinds of fish, 18 species of bivalves and 250 species of birds live in the Morro Bay estuary, the largest area of its kind left unspoiled on the West Coast.*

32

Their presence in nearby Montaña de Oro State Park has created an enchanted forest, a refuge for numerous creatures from the elusive early-morning surfer to the even more elusive Monarch butterfly.

A refuge for wildlife, domesticated life and a few things in-between: that's what Morro Bay and its neighbor communities of Baywood Park and Los Osos are all about. Which leads us to the Morro Bay estuary. Here, in this low-key meeting place of fresh and salt water, millions of organisms find a congenial place to live. Some – like the thousands of migratory birds – are as temporary as summer vacationers. Others – like the gawky geoduck clam – call these 1,500 acres home.

33

34

*The rainbowed sea: treasures at the end of the rainbow off the coast include the koala-like sea otter, who eats, plays, mates and sleeps in the sea. In his marine waterbed, the otter (pictured below) uses kelp as a tie-fast and a blanket. Pictured right, top to bottom: rainbow colors below the sea's surface include brittle stars, a polka-dotted nudibranch and a sea anemone.*

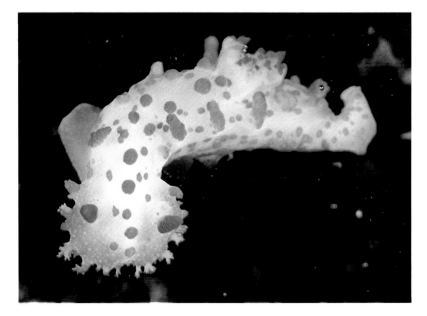

If Morro Bay could boast nothing more than the estuary, it would be wealthy. But it also has 581-foot Morro Rock; the sand spit, a long digit of land that stretches rolling white dunes toward the Rock; and the twin wonders of two state parks. Among its tall trees, Morro Bay State Park harbors herons and butterflies as well as RVs. Montaña de Oro State Park has coves to beachcomb, mountains to climb, horse trails to ride, dunes to picnic, deer to spot – in short, it's the Compleat semi-wild park.

All along the coast, there's a beach – and a park – for every taste. Frisbee-throwers and picture-takers favor Atascadero State Beach, just north of Morro Rock. Pier fishermen and surfers often choose Cayucos. Further north begin the beaches of Cambria and San Simeon, attractive to rockhounds, driftwood pickers and sea otter watchers. Good vantage points for otter-spotting are near Morro Rock, along Moonstone Beach Drive and just south of Piedras Blancas lighthouse.

35

*Renaissance of the ab: Cayucos is also the home of a thriving abalone farm, the only commercial source of the meaty mollusk. Once so plentiful that divers were paid 20¢ a dozen for them, abalones of legal eating size have become very scarce in the wild.*

36

It's not just the beaches that distinguish one coastal community from another. The towns themselves have personalities and surroundings as sharply distinct as good cheese. Which seems appropriate, since the entire area was settled in the mid-1800s by Italian-Swiss dairying families.

Famous for its long fishing wharf, Cayucos began as a shipping point. Back in the "butter days," large quantities of dairy and beef products were shipped from its piers and that of San Simeon.

Between Cayucos and Cambria, the hills get green and fat in winter, the color of buttermilk in summer. As a meaningful way to honor this dairying history, you might stop and eat some ice cream at the half-pint hamlet of Harmony.

Settled by quicksilver miners and lumbermen, Cambria is now an art colony with an intense cultural life, located in the dappled shadow of great gaunt pines. The town possesses great architectural variety, from English whimsy to redwoodsy Western, culminating in the outrageous and gorgeous specimens along Bridge Street.

If Hearst Castle had anything

*Blue skies: the county's 20 inches of rain per year fall dependably in the winter months, bringing sunshine much of the time to the coast. Pictured right: the Cass House in Cayucos, a delightfully grizzled specimen that was the home of Captain James Cass, town founder in the 1860s.*

as unpretentious as a front porch, San Simeon would be it. Once a whaling port, San Simeon still possesses mementos of those roistering days on display at Sebastian's Store, itself a State Historical Landmark.

North of San Simeon stands the slender column of Piedras Blancas (White Rocks) lighthouse. Among the dangers it illuminates offshore are three rocky islets, frosted white as wedding cake from centuries of bird deposits. Besides its automated warning functions, Piedras Blancas serves as a base for marine wildlife studies.

# HEARST CASTLE

*A man's dream, a woman's doing,
built and rebuilt
into a shimmer of hilltop towers
the splendor of those golden days
untarnished still.*

*A castle from scratch:* when building began in 1919, there was scant vegetation or topsoil on the hill. The builders had to haul a mountain of soil from the alluvial lowlands of the ranch before planting could even start. Eventually the hill was made enchanted with grapevines, thousands of flower bushes and over 100,000 trees.

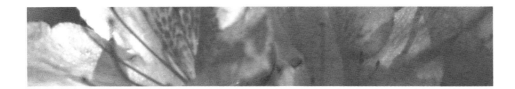

As seasoned travelers know, approaches are often as important as destinations. Take Hearst Castle, for instance. Flying into San Luis Obispo County from the north is the grand way, the fitting way, the altogether Hearstian way to get your first look at the place. Book a late afternoon flight if possible. That way, you fly over the splendid wildness of Big Sur when the sun falls with maximum drama on the deeply furrowed Santa Lucia Mountains. Mile after mile, they scissor down to the ocean, suddenly to end near Ragged Point. From this point south, the land wipes its face clean. You glide over baby-smooth cheeks of grassy plain, unreal in its perfection. A few cattle pock the surface, reminders of the area's cattle ranch days.

Then you see Hearst Castle, rearing up like a stallion, its slender white towers echoed by the exclamation points of tall palms. At the base of its 1,600-foot hill is San Simeon Point, dipping its wooded green glove into the Pacific. Its pier was the point of entry for nearly every stick, stone and antique at the Castle. (The items that did not come by boat had an equally complex trip by rail to San Luis Obispo and on to San Simeon by truck.)

If you have the time, follow your Hearst Castle tours with a visit to San Simeon. Stroll along the beach and try to visualize those enormous fireplaces you just saw, those carved ceilings you just admired, landing at that little pier, traveling up a narrow road, and being reassembled into what you see today.

Only when you realize that all of it — from the building and road materials on down — was delivered in this arduous fashion, can you gain an appreciation of the grandeur and guts of this endeavor.

41

*The glory days: William Randolph Hearst (pictured bottom right with Marion Davies in the 1930s) liked the idea of using talented craftsmen to produce items that would mesh well with his antique and art purchases. In some instances, their abilities were such that the copies are difficult to tell from the originals. Items such as the tiles that ornamented the risers of the stairways were made especially for the castle.*

42

Why did William Randolph Hearst choose this remote spot for his dream castle? The story begins with Hearst's parents. In 1865, his father George, a Missourian who made his fortune in the gold and silver fields of California, started buying land along this part of the coast. He first purchased part of the 40,000-acre Rancho Piedra Blanca. Over the years, George Hearst added land until his holdings amounted to a small kingdom. On this huge cattle ranch William Randolph Hearst and his parents spent their summers, pitching tents on the promontory called "Camp Hill." As a boy, WRH also spent much time in Europe with his art-loving mother Phoebe. There his own art collection and appreciation began.

WRH grew up to become a successful publisher and pioneer

film-maker. In 1903, he married and in due course had five sons of his own to take camping. In 1919, his mother died and Hearst inherited the vast holdings of "the ranch." It was about then that he got the notion of building something a little more permanent on Camp Hill.

Simple things have a way of snowballing, especially if fate brings the right people together.

Through his mother, William Randolph Hearst had been lucky enough to connect with San Francisco architect Julia Morgan. The pair had already worked together on other Hearst family projects.

Now they embarked on San Simeon. Originally, WRH had a modest bungalow in mind, an idea rapidly discarded in favor of a grander vision. His ideas and

Morgan's ability to interpret them produced an increasingly elaborate, ever-evolving complex of buildings. And *how* they evolved. Hearst Castle cost millions and remained unfinished even at WRH's death in 1951, primarily because of the modifications. For example, the Neptune Pool was rebuilt twice before Hearst was satisfied with it. The completed towers of Casa Grande, the main building, were once lifted to add a fourth floor. Changes like that were legion. Sometimes they were made to incorporate new art treasures Hearst had acquired. Other times, to explore an architectural alternative. Yet the Castle complex – the 100-room Casa Grande and the three guest houses around it – remained coherent and pleasing, a tribute to Morgan's rare ability to synthesize.

There are superlatives and statistics enough at Hearst Castle to satisfy the most ravenous *"Ripley's Believe-it-or-Not"* reader. The ranch produced a large portion of its own foodstuffs, especially fresh meat. Besides livestock, you could just as easily bump into a zebra or a tiger. Hearst once owned the largest private zoo in the world, with more than 100 species on the grounds.

Hearst spared nothing to please his guests. They could choose to swim in either of two pools, containing more than half a million gallons of water; go riding; play tennis or billiards; or see first-run films. WRH supplied every amenity: bathing suits, tennis clothes, riding habits – even fur coats!

If you were in the mood for counting, at Hearst Castle you would find: 49 bathrooms, 58 bedrooms and two libraries with more than 10,000 books. You could also check on the 2,144 rose bushes and admire the cypresses, which were hauled to the site full-grown.

Ultimately, Hearst Castle became more than the sum of its extraordinary parts. Begun as a bungalow, the castle on La Cuesta Encantada grew into a rich man's showplace, an artistic monument and a living museum. Upon Hearst's death, his castle was given to the people of California and assumed its final role. As a state historical monument, the castle on the Enchanted Hill now casts its spell over millions of visitors each year.

45

*All that glitters: it took artisans five years to hand-set the gold leaf and more than half a million mosaic tiles in the Roman Pool, pictured bottom. Restoration and maintenance of Hearst Castle continues to absorb state funds annually. Pictured top: Hearst's third-floor Gothic Study, at one time the nerve center of his publishing empire.*

# NORTH COUNTY

*Over the grade, the land shows its muscle*
*a horizon of hills, tattooed with rocks*
*great oaks and grapevines*
*bursting like biceps from the earth*
*toward skies of stone-washed denim.*

To get to know what we call "North County," pick a fall day, any day — they're all as crisp and tangy as local apples. Start in San Luis Obispo city and drive north over Cuesta Grade on Highway 101. It's only a 1,550-foot climb, but what a difference those 1,550 feet make. You see it at once in the terrain. Lush greenery gives way to grasslands and oaks. You can feel it too: the hot is hotter; the cold, colder; the dry, dryer.

It's tempting to get off the main road at once. This trip, persevere until the Highway 46 east turnoff. Immediately you plunge into wine country. Wineries like Martin, Eberle, Estrella and Arciero line the road. There are dozens of other wineries and vineyards in North County, of course. But to see the array along Highway 46 is to grasp the scope of the industry. We're talking thousands of acres of grapes. Prime grapes, bending the vines with their clusters. From the road you can see them gleaming with the dusty bloom they acquire just before harvest. (Romantic-looking bloom is actually wild yeast, the agent that causes grapes to ferment.)

You could spend all day just moseying from tasting-room to tasting-room. But there are other things to look at: fields of grain, almonds, cattle. Near the county's eastern border, you encounter Cholame and the meeting-place of Highways 46 and 41, where actor James Dean was killed in 1955. His fans continue to visit this spot, now embellished with a memorial built by a Japanese businessman. Beneath this small intersection lies a meeting-place of another sort: the San Andreas fault. Along its 700-mile length, two tectonic plates rub against one another, from time to time relieving their tension with an earthquake.

49

*Solid gold: spring safflowers, summer sun through a catamaran sail at Lake Nacimiento, and an autumn portrait of a Shandon pioneer.*

*Bright reminder of an adventurous age:* luck and isolation may have preserved Mission San Miguel Arcangel. Especially beautiful are its interior frescoes and the wall-pulpit with its dove. Isolation also attracted the lawless to the area, from the James brothers to the Daltons. In 1848, the mission was secularized and bought by a family named Reed. A short time later, all eleven Reeds were found murdered. A vigilante party overtook the killers near Santa Barbara; three of the bandits' bodies now lie in the mission cemetery.

51

earthquakes were nothing new to the Franciscan fathers who settled this area in 1797. By that time, Father Junípero Serra and his followers had established 15 missions in Alta California. Mission San Miguel was the beneficiary of their experience; it survived the great quakes of 1812 and 1857 with little damage.

In its heyday, the 16th mission was vital and prosperous. Its lands near the Salinas River grew wheat and grazed cattle, its Indian converts made thousands of roof tiles for this and other missions. Certainly it was – and has remained – one of the prettiest missions. San Miguel's interior, delicately painted by the Indians under the guidance of Catalan artist Estéban Munras, has had the good fortune to be preserved.

Other Indian artistic legacies have not been so lucky. To the east on Carrisa plain stands Painted Rock. This huge natural amphitheatre may have been a temple, a trade site and a fiesta place. Its 200-foot-high surfaces were once covered with glorious red, white and black pictographs painted by local tribes. Among the images they left were the two serpents that held up the world. The Indians believed that when the serpents tired, their movements made the earth quake. Now in private hands, the remnants of Painted Rock are a sad reminder of the fate of the Indians themselves.

Green hills and gold –
wherever you look in North County,
their fluted edges draw your eye,
their soft Spanish names beguile
your tongue. Hidden in the Santa
Lucias are mountain secrets: wild
turkeys, wild boar, played-out gold
mines, rare Sargent cypresses –
even oil wells, their flatulent smoke
signals neatly hidden by the
foothills around San Ardo. Further
east, you encounter the bare bones
of the Temblor Range, sitting
uneasily on the San Andreas fault.
This is cicada-dry terrain, adorned
only with a soda lake or two.

To the north and west, sweet water is abundant. At the top of the county map, a huge, splay-footed paperweight called Lake Nacimiento links San Luis Obispo and Monterey Counties. Formed by a dam on the Nacimiento River, the lake is the warm-water playground for North County. Its 165 miles of shoreline accommodate Labor Dayloads of ardent waterskiiers, boaters, campers and fisherpersons. Aficionados of smaller lakes head for Santa Margarita Lake, popular for fishing, and Atascadero Lake, headquarters for a thriving zoo.

*The lonely cerros of San Luis Obispo: "cerro" means hill in Spanish; with morro, it is often used in the naming of our modestly mountainous terrain. A century or more ago, without benefit of combustion engines, the cerros and morros seemed a lot higher. It took the coming of the Southern Pacific railroad in 1894 to effectively end the isolation of the county.*

*Bursting with pride:* the Mid-State county fair, held in Paso Robles, boasts the biggest lineup of entertainment in the U.S. Besides celebrity glitter, the fair offers an opportunity to see a superb array of ag products – from North County almonds to 4-H lambs. Pictured bottom right: an event of a different sort occurs each September 30, when James Dean admirers gather for a tribute in Cholame on the anniversary of his death.

North County raises lots of crops. Small-town friendliness is one of them. That is probably why the two-week County Fair is held in Paso Robles. A little city that came into being as a spa and stagecoach stop, Paso is the center for North County historical activities as well as its agricultural focus. Each fall, Paso hosts the Pioneer Day dustup. On that day, every ancient rig and wrangler who is able to move, does so. The result is an astonishing parade of machines, horseflesh and men.

The largest city in North County is Atascadero, a model community developed in 1913 by E.G. Lewis. About the only vestige of Lewis' era is the Administration building, a handsome Italian Renaissance structure.

Like their larger counterparts, Templeton, Santa Margarita and San Miguel have a homespun Western quality. They are places where cowboy hats are not an affectation but everyday wear. Just as rewarding are the truly tiny towns: Creston and Shandon, Pozo and Rinconada.

But the biggest charm of North County remains the great breathing spaces between its towns and villages. Sometimes connected by a small road, sometimes by nothing at all, the hills and plains offer a vivid and changing calendar to the curious.

Paradise, however, has its problems, the worst of which is drought, followed by fire. To the outsider, the periodic fires which burn large portions of California down to charred ash would seem to be catastrophic. From man's standpoint, they are. But Nature is more resourceful. The intense heat of a huge blaze – such as the 1985 Las Pilitas fire – has a catalytic action on the seeds hidden in the earth. The spring following a fire is often the most beautiful of the decade, the meadows and slopes aflame with wildflowers that were awakened by the fire's heat.

*Flowering phoenix: the year following a fire – such as the Las Pilitas burns of 1921 and 1985 – finds an incandescent display of poppies and other wildflowers among the the blackened fingers of the manzanita shrubs. Many seeds are triggered only by the heat of a large fire. Other reasons to travel east in North County: the wacky little ghost town of Rinconada and the Pozo Saloon, both found along Pozo Road.*

# SOUTH COUNTY

*Sun-warmed soil, flower-striped,*
*fragrant with eucalyptus*
*edged with beaches*
*whose skirts of sand*
*trail in the long lace of waves.*

**Back in time:** *South County is hip-deep in grand old Victorians, vernacular architecture of all sorts and nostalgia – such as Young Louis' collection of antique cameras. Louis, pictured left, is the son of Ah Louis, Chinese entrepreneur who began the local flower seed industry, among other things.*

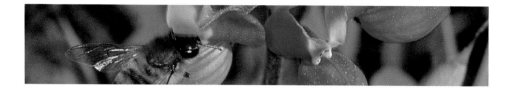

South County has a nostalgic, Ray Bradbury feeling to it, the look of a land where you'd like your kids to grow up. Or maybe to stay kids forever. It's hard to define where South County begins. But it's easy to describe one of the most enchanting ways to get there.

Start at the south edge of San Luis Obispo city, and follow the pretty little snake called Orcutt Road as it curves serpentinely around Islay Hill, making its way down Edna Valley. Driving Orcutt can be a menace. Besides watching out for joggers, bikers, horseback riders and other slow-moving frequenters of Orcutt, you are constantly being seduced by the changing views, both front and back. With each twist of the road, the volcanic peaks of the county (of which Islay Hill is one) rearrange themselves into pleasing new patterns. All around you are miles of rollercoaster vineyards, presided over by huge birds of prey. Minute sideroads beckon. Interesting old buildings call out to be photographed. You could just mooch along all day, pausing at a winery or two for replenishment of necessary body fluids.

If, however, you insist on a destination, then turn right at Biddle Ranch Road to get to Highway 227; just one of three beautiful routes to reach the village of Arroyo Grande and nearby Lopez Lake.

This is horse country. You pass farm after farm of Arabians, lifting their expensive eyebrows at you from impeccable fields of juicy green. If you can swing it, explore this route on horseback yourself. That way, you'll get to take in the varied textures and flavors of the road. And you'll get to do the most evocative South County thing of all: ride through forests of eucalyptus, letting your horse's hooves bite into the aromatic leaves on the ground to send their dizzying, dusty perfume up to you.

61

63

*Salt water, fresh water: with all that ocean offshore, you tend to overlook the county's lakes – ten square miles of them. South County's biggest is Lopez Lake, a warm-water aquamarine in a jade setting. Oso Flaco ("lean bear") Lake is the largest of the lakes that hide among the Oceano sand dunes.*

All the horsey activity is not confined to this area, of course. But much of the topography and vegetation of South County – the broad sand-duned beaches, the eucalyptus forests of Nipomo Mesa – seems to encourage pleasure riding.

Sand is grand, and South County has lots of it. It also has large quantities of the most fertile soil in the county, centered around the Arroyo Grande Valley. Along parts of Highway 1, you see the earth, rich and black as French roast coffee, that first drew agricultural attention back in the 1700s. At that time, the Franciscan fathers at Mission San Luis Obispo established a garden in this fertile bottomland. Later settlers, such as William Dana and Francisco Branch, were also magnetized by the soil's possibilities, which produced vegetables and fruit of prodigious size and vigor. (The annual Harvest Festival winners have included 50-pound cabbages, 19-pound carrots and a beet over seven feet long.) Locals love South County produce for its flavor also; the strawberries are particularly famous.

Surrounded by farms and flower fields, Arroyo Grande is the oldest and largest town in South County yet retains a distinct village character. Along Grand Avenue, its main artery, Arroyo Grande is linked to its companion villages, Grover City and Oceano.

East of Arroyo Grande you encounter the Santa Lucia Wilderness, the intensely emerald contours of Lopez Canyon with its waterfalls big and small, and a watery jewel called Lopez Lake. Lopez has 22 miles of shoreline, warm-water swimming, excellent wind-surfing and trout fishing.

Tucked away behind a bird-beak of land whose eye is the lighthouse at Port San Luis, Avila Beach gets the lion's share of sunny beach days along our coast. That fact, coupled with its slightly raffish beach-bum air and its hot springs, give Avila a strong Southern California feeling. The sleepy Southern California, that is, of 30 years ago.

Unpretentious pleasures are Avila's specialty. That might mean a nighttime hot-dog roast on the beach; Mexican-style seafood at a local institution; or a sunset swim and soak at the hot springs. There's nothing quite like floating on your back at the hot springs, gazing at the palm trees that frame the pool

and watching the steam off your body make sulphurous contrails toward a sky of deep blue velvet.

Other downhome local pleasures include weekend trips to nearby See Canyon to taste the new cider and buy apples. Narrow enough to get the cold nights necessary for superior apple growing, See Canyon produces dozens of unusual apple varieties.

As if more treats were needed, you can also drive through See Canyon to experience the most exhilarating itinerary in the county: the 10½-mile, merry-go-round

climb up and down Prefumo Canyon. It begins quietly enough. The road soon turns washboardlike, so rough that you start thinking somehow you drove off on your rims. Two people are needed on a Prefumo Canyon run – one to drive one to gawk. Once you stop to picnic, you have a view of Morro Rock and nearly all the peaks. On a clear day, you can see north to Whale Rock and beyond. Turn the other direction, and you glimpse the great white swath of beaches that run clear to Pt. Sal and the Santa Barbara County line.

*Small-town pleasures: shrimp tacos along Avila's boardwalk; fresh fish caught from the pier; dream waves at Pismo; a boat trip to the lighthouse at Port San Luis.*

South of the Avila headlands begin the sea-nibbled cliffs of Shell Beach. Named for the shell mounds left in abundance by the Chumash Indians, Shell Beach perches high above a narrow but attractive strip of sand. You reach the beach via a series of steep and scenic stairways. Once there, you have lots to explore. The hungry sea has eaten away at the caramel-colored cliffs to such an extent that they are honeycombed with archways, caves, tunnels and formations of every description. Some of the access points offer fine tidepool and seal observation, too.

Further south at Pismo Beach, the cliffs at water's edge disappear and the sliver of beach widens to a huge slice of sand. The Pismo dunes are brilliant white, made even whiter by the burning reds, oranges and pinks of Pismo's lusty population of geraniums, nasturtiums and iceplant.

For centuries, this area was popular with the Chumash. They loved the clams found in such abundance. And they loved the odd black stuff – so convenient for canoe-sealing – that oozed out of the sand. The Indians called it *pizmu*; we call it tar, and you still see an occasional blob of it on the beach. Not so, unfortunately, with the Pismo clam, once so plentiful it was used for fertilizer. In this

*Of dunes and men*: *a small Sahara of dunes rolls south from Pismo past Oceano and along the Nipomo Mesa. Their curves conceal rare flowers, such as the giant coreopsis, pictured top center; shell mounds or middens, the remains of long-ago Indian feasts; and a variety of interesting plants and animals. What you won't find among the dunes – or anywhere on the beach – are mature Pismo clams. In the early years of the 20th century, the daily limit was 200 clams per person. On big weekends, as many as 25,000 clams were taken. Pleasure digging is still allowed but it's rare to uncover a clam that meets the legal limit of 4½."*

century, the Pismo population has been subjected to pressure from both human and animal predators. Net result: almost no clams.

Near Pismo, the beach is flat and accessible for driving. Then it begins to pick up momentum and the great dunes begin – twelve miles of them, undulating all the way to Pt. Sal. A chunk called the Pismo Dunes State Vehicle Recreation Area has been set aside for dune buggies and other bumptious vehicles. This area apart, you can easily be as alone as you like in a whispering sea of sand. Free to happen upon the explosive yellow flowers of the rare giant coreopsis. Or to sit and gaze at the birds on Oso Flaco Lake. Or to watch in wonder as the Monarch butterflies migrate to the eucalyptus trees that flank the dunes.

All butterflies – Monarchs included – owe their colors and their ability to fly to pigment scales as fine as dust. Be less than gentle with a Monarch, and you not only dim his colors but cripple him as well. This county – beneficiary of so much beauty – needs the same butterfly touch. To keep this environment in fragile balance, we must learn to leave things be. To do more looking. To do less doing. And our visitors have the same responsibility as the residents. We love our county: please SLO down.

*Halcyon days: one of South County's hidden treasures is a settlement called Halcyon, an oasis of tranquility and beauty that seems to personify the most desirable qualities of this whole area. At its center, Halcyon has a noble structure called the Temple of the People, built by the theosophical sect of the same name. Like the Monarch butterflies that roost in its tall trees, Halcyon is fragile. Look your fill, but please don't touch.*

# INDEX & RESOURCE GUIDE

• San Luis Obispo County Visitors and Conference Bureau: 1041 Chorro, Suite E, San Luis Obispo: 541-8000.

• Arroyo Grande Chamber: 200 E. Branch, Arroyo Grande: 489-1488.

• Atascadero Chamber: 6550 El Camino Real, Atascadero: 466-2044.

• Cambria Chamber: 767 Main, Cambria: 927-3624.

• Cayucos Chamber: 151 Cayucos Dr., Cayucos: 995-1200.

• Grover City Chamber: 177 S. 8th, Grover City: 489-9091.

• Los Osos-Baywood Park Chamber: 900 Los Osos Valley Rd., Los Osos: 528-4884.

• Morro Bay Chamber: 385 Morro Bay Blvd., Morro Bay: 772-4467.

• Paso Robles Chamber: 1113 Spring, Paso Robles: 238-0506.

• Pismo Beach Chamber: 581 Dolliver, Pismo Beach: 773-4382.

• San Luis Obispo City Chamber: 1039 Chorro, San Luis Obispo: 543-1323.

• San Simeon Chamber: Highway 1, San Simeon: 927-3500.

• Templeton Chamber: 5th & Paso Robles, Templeton: 434-1789.

*This is a partial list only. For further information, please contact the Chambers of Commerce listed above:*

• Feb: Mardi Gras in San Luis Obispo and Pismo Beach.

• April: the university's Poly Royal celebration in San Luis Obispo.

• May: La Fiesta in San Luis Obispo; the Paso Robles Wine Festival; the Arroyo Grande Strawberry Festival.

• June: Renaissance Faire in San Luis Obispo.

• July: 4th of July festivities and fireworks in various towns; Obon Festival in San Luis Obispo.

• Aug: Mozart Festival, held county-wide; Mid-State County Fair in Paso Robles; Pinedorado in Cambria; Central Coast Wine Festival in San Luis Obispo.

• Sept: Mission San Miguel Fiesta in San Miguel; Firemen's Muster in Morro Bay; Harvest Festival in Arroyo Grande.

• Oct: Harbor Festival in Morro Bay; Pioneer Day in Paso Robles; Colony Days in Atascadero.

• Nov: Clam Festival in Pismo Beach.

Farmers' Markets .............. 7, 9, 1[

• *Call the local chambers to confirm day[ and times and for specific directions:*

• Arroyo Grande: Wednesday evening i[ two locations.

• Atascadero: Wednesday evening.

• Paso Robles: Thursday evening.

• Morro Bay: Thursday late afternoon.

• San Luis Obispo city: held in two locations on Saturday morning and Thursday evening. The evening Farmers' Market is the most elaborate in the county, combining fresh produce with entertainment and outdoor barbecuing in a pedestrian-only downtown setting.

• Templeton: Saturday afternoon.

Cover:

How to have a peak experience: the view
from San Luis Mountain looking seaward
gives you a grand gander at Bishop's
Peak, Chumash Peak, Cerro Romauldo
and Hollister Peak. Some sunsets are
luckier than others; in this one, you can
see the hemisphere of Morro Rock, slightly to the south of Hollister.
*Photo by Tony Hertz.*

# SAN LUIS OBISPO COUNTY...

# CALIFORNIA'S BEST-KEPT SECRET